TENNIS HEALTH
A GUIDE FOR TENNIS INJURY PREVENTION AND REHABILITATION

CASEY L. DEATON, MPT

Bloomington, IN Milton Keynes, UK

AuthorHouse™
1663 Liberty Drive, Suite 200
Bloomington, IN 47403
www.authorhouse.com
Phone: 1-800-839-8640

AuthorHouse™ UK Ltd.
500 Avebury Boulevard
Central Milton Keynes, MK9 2BE
www.authorhouse.co.uk
Phone: 08001974150

© *2007 Casey L. Deaton, MPT. All rights reserved.*

No part of this book may be reproduced, stored in a retrieval system, or transmitted by any means without the written permission of the author.

First published by AuthorHouse 8/21/2007

ISBN: 978-1-4259-9188-3 (sc)

Printed in the United States of America
Bloomington, Indiana

This book is printed on acid-free paper.

CONTENTS

INTRODUCTION	vii
TERMINOLOGY	ix
CONCEPTS OF TENNIS HEALTH	1
PRINCIPLES OF STRETCHING AND STRENGTHENING	3
JOINT SPECIFIC FUNCTION, ANATOMY AND EXERCISES	9
SHOULDER	10
ELBOW AND WRIST	24
THE SPINE	31
THE HIP AND KNEE	45
THE FOOT AND ANKLE	66
INJURY IDENTIFICATION	81
WHEN INJURIES OCCUR	85
KEY POINTS TO BETTER TENNIS HEALTH	91

INTRODUCTION

The sport of tennis is, for many, an ideal way to stay fit, socialize with friends, live out competitive desires, and for a select few to enhance their livelihood. From young to old, male or female, it is an important part of exercise routines and general overall well-being. Thus, tennis can be an integral part of maintaining not only physical health, but also one's emotional and psychological health. Therefore, to stay active and involved in tennis is much more than mere recreation.

Regardless of a person's age, gender or skill level, a certain degree of physical health is needed not only to progress and succeed in the sport of tennis, but also to simply participate. When injuries occur, the participant's performance and possibly even their ability to participate at all can be significantly reduced. Staying "tennis fit" is an essential part of maintaining one's physical ability to carry out activities required to participate in this great sport. This involves resolving current or ongoing pains, and more importantly, preparing the body for such specific tasks. Thus, it is imperative to better train one's muscles and joints to adequately handle the rigors of tennis, thus ensuring prolonged participation in this lifelong sport. Consequently, not only is injury rehabilitation an important aspect of tennis health, but possibly more so is injury prevention.

This booklet is designed to educate the average tennis athlete on involved anatomy, function of joints during tennis activities, targeting pain complaints and improving conditioning of these tissues for tennis participation. It will also address the management of an injury once it is detected. It is by no means an exhaustive manual for complete tennis health, but should be a good tool in injury prevention and preparation of the athlete for lifelong tennis enjoyment.

TERMINOLOGY

Throughout this book several important anatomical and medical terms will be used. Here is a list of these words along with definitions to assist with comprehension of information.

Arthritis: the wearing down or degeneration of the surfaces that make up joints.

Bursitis: irritation or inflammation of fluid filled sacs near joints.

Cartilage: the protective tissue within joints where joint movement occurs.

Extension: the motion of a joint in a straightening direction. Extensors: the muscles responsible for creating extension motion.

Flexibility: the length of a particular muscle, which allows joints to move through a certain amount of motion.

Flexion: the motion of a joint in a bending direction. Flexors: the muscles responsible for creating flexion motion.

Fracture: injury to the bone resulting in breakage.

Ligament: firm tissue around joints that promote stability and prevent unwanted joint motions.

Meniscus: Cartilage-like tissues within the knee joints that provide shock absorption and stability to the knees.

Muscle: tissues that contract or activate to perform desired movements in a joint.

Muscle endurance: the ability of a muscle to exert force over many repetitions.

Muscle strength: the amount of force a muscle can produce.

Orthotic: an external device used to assist with joint, muscle/tendon, or ligament support, stability, or force reduction.

Rotation: the motion of a joint in a twisting direction. External Rotation: rotating away from body. Internal Rotation: rotating towards body.

Sprain: injury sustained to ligaments, which can vary from small to large tears.

Stability: the process by which the ligaments, muscles and tendons around a joint maintain normal joint positioning during stressful movements.

Strain: injury sustained to muscle, which can vary from small to large tears.

Tendon: firm tissue which connects muscle to bone.

Tendonitis: irritation or inflammation of tissue which attaches muscle to bone.

CONCEPTS OF TENNIS HEALTH

When performing repetitive physical activities such as those required by tennis, the body is subject to two types of problems: overuse injuries and acute injuries. Overuse injuries refer to injuries that develop over time. This means that relatively forceful motions produced at certain body parts can impart cumulative stresses on the tissues in that body part. If these tissues are not healthy or conditioned enough to properly tolerate such repetitive motions, they can break down over time. This can result in lingering soreness, pain, swelling or more serious types of injury, which in turn can impair one's performance and possibly even participation for indefinite amounts of time. Such types of overuse injuries are tendonitis or bursitis, which commonly involves shoulder and elbow musculature, and even arthritis, which is wearing down of protective cartilage within joints. The other noted injury is an acute injury. This happens with a single traumatic event disrupting the stability of a particular joint by damage to muscle, tendon, ligament or bone. Such examples of acute injuries may be ankle sprains, hamstring strains, or fractures.

The body needs a certain amount of muscle symmetry or balance to be able to tolerate activities required by tennis or to prevent onsets of injury. Balance of muscle strength and flexibility around joints are necessary. During activities requiring repetitive forceful motions, such as in tennis, muscles on both sides of the joint are very important. While one set of muscles contract to create the motion, the opposing set is utilized to provide stability to the joint as well as to slow the motion when completed. If strength on both sides is not proportional, irregular stresses are placed on the tissues, thus predisposing one for tendonitis or strain types of problems. Also, if flexibility is not sufficient on both sides of the joint, a full and adequate range of motion of the joint can be inhibited. As a result, excessive muscle effort is required to counter the tightness that can occur. When continuous unequal forces are placed on joint surfaces over time due to strength or flexibility imbalances, it causes wear and tear to the joint surfaces or articular cartilage. This contributes to the breaking down or degeneration of the joint surfaces known as arthritis. By maintaining a balance of muscle strength and flexibility on either side of joints, it enables equal stress to be imparted on involved joints, which prevents abnormal or uneven stresses on the muscles, tendons, ligaments and the joint surfaces itself. It is when these repetitive forces are abnormally transferred through these tissues and joints that breakdown or injury can occur.

Acute injuries are also limited or prevented by muscle balance around joints. During tennis participation the body is required to make quick, forceful accelerations, decelerations, or changes in direction. These quick changes place strong forces on involved joints, thus demanding good stability in these joints to be able to handle such forces. This stability comes from both the ligaments and muscles around the joint. If the muscles surrounding the joint are strengthened adequately, they can easily accommodate and counter these forces, thus preventing any excessive motion of the joint or undue stress to the muscles themselves.

PRINCIPLES OF STRETCHING AND STRENGTHENING

Warm up: in order for muscles and tendons to respond appropriately and safely to exercise, a brief warm up should be performed. This warm up should be light repetitive activity designed to increase blood flow to target tissues and increase heart rate. This activity will make muscles and tendons more receptive to stretching and strengthening, as well as help transition into more vigorous activity. Typical warm ups may be light jogging, bike riding, arm circles. Failure to warm up muscles properly may result in excessive stress to cold muscles, thus hindering response to activity or also predisposing for injury.

Examples of warm ups: shoulder circles, squatting, jogging in place, leg swings.

shoulder circles

squatting

jogging in place

leg swings

Stretching:

Stretching is the act of lengthening muscles and their tendons to allow joints (which these muscles and tendons cross) to move through a full and adequate range of motion necessary for a particular activity. If these muscles and tendons are not flexible enough to accommodate the specific motion required by joints used in tennis, then excessive stress can build on these tissues and lead to poor performance or injury. Stretching is also effective after sport performance in reducing muscle soreness by assisting in removal of lactic acid. Lactic acid is a byproduct of muscle exertion during activity, which when accumulated in muscles can cause a "burning" sensation and fatigue.

2 Types of stretching include: dynamic stretching and static stretching.

Dynamic stretching: This is wide ranging repetitive motion through specific joints to target muscles and tendons. It is generally not as effective as static stretching, but is very useful as a warm up. Such stretching activity should be performed for approximately 30 sec. Examples are shoulder and leg swings.

Static stretching: This is the most common form of stretching. It requires placing a muscle on a light to moderate stretch and holding for a prescribed period of time. This better allows for muscle and tendon fibers to elongate, thus improving length or flexibility of this muscle.

General guidelines for effective static stretching:

- Perform 3 to 5 stretches to each muscle and maintain this stretch for 12-15 seconds.

- Stretches should be relaxed and comfortable. If too aggressive of a stretch is performed, the muscles are likely to remain tense and not allow for a proper elongation.

- Light to moderate stretching should be performed for about 5 minutes before activity or tennis in order to warm up and prepare for sport. Dynamic stretching is effective at this time.

- Slightly more aggressive static stretching should be performed after activity or sport since muscles and tendons are warm and more receptive to stretch. This will also help to reduce muscle soreness.

Strengthening:

Strengthening is the act of applying resisted forces to muscles and tendons to improve force of muscle output through specific joints. Most commonly, strengthening is associated with improving power with sport performance. This is accurate, but strengthening is also vital in improving muscle and tendon strength for joint stability, which is essential in tennis. An important concept of strengthening that is often overlooked is functional strengthening, which requires strengthening tissues specifically for whatever physical endeavor one is participating in. In tennis, maximum strength is not required one or two times; moderate strength is required continually over many repetitions. This ability for our muscles to produce these moderately strong forces time and time again is referred to as muscle endurance. Also, our muscles need to be able to create stability around our joints by holding the joint surfaces in correct positions, thus allowing for proper production of these forces over many repetitions.

General guidelines for effective functional strengthening specific for tennis performance:

- Perform 15-30 repetitions of a specific exercise beginning with 2 sets and progressing to 4 sets.

- The resistance utilized should be light enough to allow for completion of 15-30 repetitions per set with mild fatigue. "Burn out" or point of full fatigue is <u>not</u> necessary. Resistance should be increased when performing 20-30 repetitions easily. Also, progressions with exercise techniques should only be attempted once prior technique is mastered.

- Exercises should be performed through full range of motion with a controlled speed at a particular joint, thus strengthening the full muscle and encouraging flexibility.

- Resistance utilized can include body weight, free weights, weight machines, and resistive bands or cords. Photographs of exercises will be given providing examples of each.

JOINT SPECIFIC FUNCTION, ANATOMY AND EXERCISES

This section will address important structures of the primary joints in the body related to tennis play. It will describe the roles of these structures in tennis participation and how to properly condition them to allow for optimal joint health. It will also educate on the factors that contribute to the most common tennis related injuries and how to interpret your symptoms for targeting problems.

For each body part, a thorough set of exercises will be given to address optimally conditioning essential structures of the tennis body. The purpose of these exercises is not only for enhanced performance, but more significantly for injury prevention. With performance of these exercises, temporary soreness may be expected; however, if performing these exercises becomes painful, stopping this particular exercise is warranted.

SHOULDER

The shoulder is one of the most important joints in tennis participation. The shoulder enables you to produce force over many different arm positions in order to accomplish a variety of shots. The reason it is effective in allowing many different positions is that inherently it is a very flexible joint. However, by being such a flexible joint, it does sacrifice stability. The shoulder's stability is enhanced by the rotator cuff. The rotator cuff is a set of four muscles: the supraspinatus, infraspinatus, subscapularis and teres minor. These muscles are designed to work together to promote stability in the shoulder joint. These are not the glorified muscles of bodybuilders, but undeniably more important. If these muscles are not conditioned adequately, force output will be less and excessive stress will be placed on the shoulder complex. Utilization of one's arm in tennis will be very ineffective and likely painful. Also, since most all of the strokes in tennis are produced in a forward direction, there is a tendency for chest muscles to become stronger and tighter than muscles near the shoulder blade (scapula), which oppose this motion. These shoulder blade muscles are very important in that they stabilize your shoulder blade to provide a stable base for your arm to move. Without a stable base, the shoulder muscles will move inefficiently and have to overwork to accomplish a desired goal. Thus, it is key to maintain good flexibility in your chest and adequate strengthening in your shoulder blade musculature.

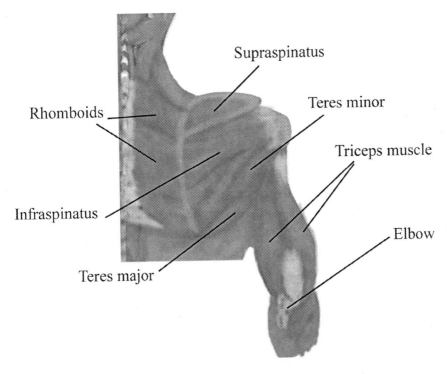

Shoulder anatomy

Complaints associated with shoulder problems:

- Rotator cuff tendonitis/biceps tendonitis: overuse inflammation or irritation to rotator cuff/biceps muscles or tendons caused by strength imbalance in rotator cuff or poor technique. Continually striking the ball behind one's body on serves or overheads is an example of poor technique that could stress the rotator cuff. (Contact should be made slightly in front of the body with these two strokes). This injury is characterized by a dull-aching or fatigued feeling in the shoulder after tennis, weakness noted during strokes, and pain near the top of the shoulder or front of the shoulder. Symptoms could progress to limitation of lifting arm overhead, which may indicate a rotator cuff tear.

<u>Prevention and rehabilitation considerations</u>: strengthen shoulder external rotation and shoulder blade retraction, stretch chest/pectoral muscles. Examples: pulley shoulder external rotations, machine rows and corner pectoral stretches.

- Shoulder instability, subluxation or cartilage tear: excessive flexibility or laxity in the tissues/capsule that hold the upper arm bone against the shoulder blade, or a tear to the inner surface of the joint. This is characterized by clunking or catching in the shoulder with overhead activities, as well as pain in the shoulder with overhead activity, reaching behind one's back and lifting. This is generally caused by a particular incident, such as a fall.

<u>Prevention and rehabilitation considerations</u>: strengthen shoulder in all directions, especially internal and external rotation. Examples: pulley shoulder internal and external rotations, and empty cans.

<u>Goals of shoulder stretching</u>: achieve adequate flexibility in chest (pectoral) muscles and rotator cuff muscles to allow for full shoulder motion. Please refer to the stretching guidelines.

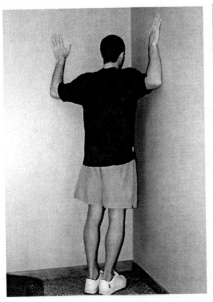 

1. Chest corner stretch- Stretches pectoral/chest muscles. Place both elbows at shoulder height against a wall on either side of a corner. Stand about 2 feet from the corner. Lean body forward. Mild stretch should be felt in chest and front of shoulders.

2. Posterior shoulder stretch- Stretches back of shoulder and muscle between shoulder blades. Pull one elbow across body using other hand until mild stretch is felt.

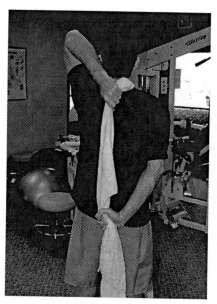 

3. Shoulder external rotator cuff stretch- Stretches external rotators of rotator cuff. Using a towel, hold one end of the towel over and behind head and other end behind back. With bottom hand, pull top hand downward. This will stretch top arm external rotators.

4. Shoulder internal rotator cuff stretch- Stretches internal rotators of rotator cuff. Using a towel, hold one end of the towel over and behind head and other end behind back. With top hand, pull bottom hand upward. This will stretch bottom arm internal rotators.

Goals of shoulder strengthening: properly condition rotator cuff muscles for shoulder strength and stabilization; strengthen shoulder blade muscles for improved base for arm motions. Please refer to the strengthening guidelines.

1a. Shoulder internal rotation strengthening at 0 degrees: Strengthens internal rotators of rotator cuff. With elbow against side as a pivot point and pulley even with the hand, pull resistance (pulley, elastic band or cord) toward your stomach, then control resistance back outward.

1b. Progression of 1a. Shoulder internal rotation strengthening in 90 degrees: Strengthens shoulder internal rotators in a more tennis specific position. Pulley position should be overhead. Place elbow out to side at shoulder height and just in front of shoulder. Pull resistance (pulley, elastic band or cord) downward, pivoting at elbow. Elbow should remain in same position. Return back to starting position.

2a. Shoulder external rotation strengthening at 0 degrees: Strengthens external rotators of rotator cuff. Begin with elbow against side, arm against stomach, and pulley even with hand. Pull resistance away from stomach by rotating outward. Then control back to starting position. Note: this may also be performed using a dumbbell by lying on opposite side, resting elbow against side and rotating arm with weight upward, keeping elbow against side.

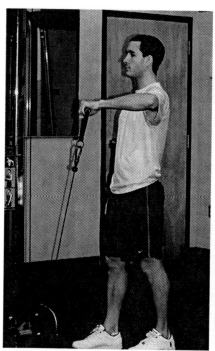 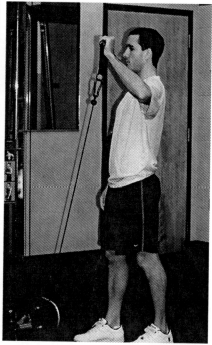

2b. Progression of 2a. Shoulder external rotation strengthening in 90 degrees: Strengthens shoulder external rotators in a more tennis specific position. Pulley should be placed at a low level. Place elbow out to side at shoulder height and just in front of shoulder. Begin with forearm just below horizontal and rotate forearm upward. Maintain elbow in constant position at shoulder height and just in front of shoulder.

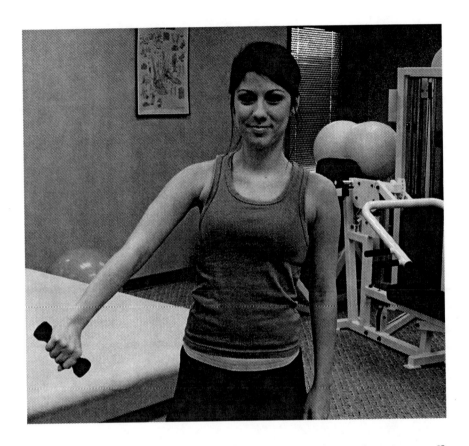

3. Empty cans: Strengthens supraspinatus muscle of rotator cuff. Begin with arm at side with thumb pointing downward. Raise arm with resistance out to the side, but slightly in front. Do not lift hand above shoulder height. Return to starting position.

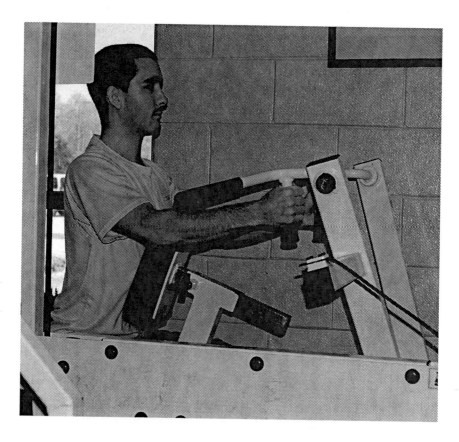

1. Rowing: Strengthens shoulder blade retraction muscles for improved shoulder stabilization. Keeping back straight, pull resistance back leading with elbow while squeezing shoulder blades together. Return to starting position.

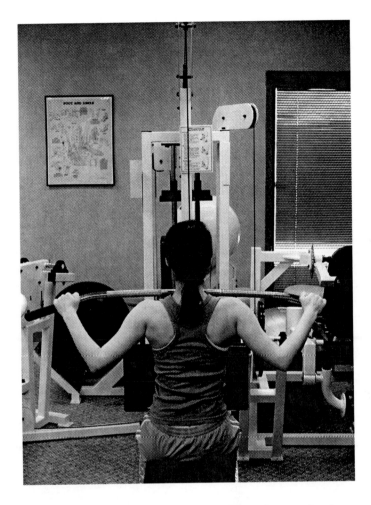

2. Lat pulldown machine: Strengthens larger back muscles, which help to stabilize the shoulder. Grasp bar at about shoulder width with palms facing away. Pull bar down toward chest, while maintaining slight arch in lower back. Return to starting position. This may also be performed with underhand grip.

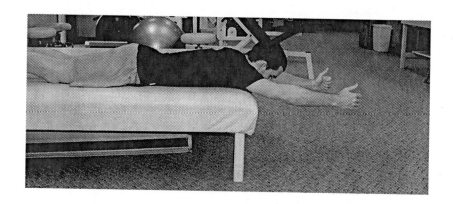

3. Shoulder Y's: Very effective with strengthening shoulder blade stabilizing muscles and neck muscles. Lie on stomach and extend arms in front in the shape of a "Y". Lift arms up off of the floor about 4-6 inches, then return to starting position. Can also be performed lying over a ball such as in following exercise. This will further strengthen back muscles. Can also utilize free weights in hands for additional resistance.

4. Shoulder T's: Very effective with strengthening shoulder blade stabilizing muscles and neck muscles. Lie on stomach and extend arms out to side with thumbs pointing upward. Lift arms up off of the floor about 4-6 inches, then return to starting position. Lying over ball as shown is progression. Can also utilize free weights in hands for additional resistance.

ELBOW AND WRIST

Here, the elbow and wrist are classified together because they share common musculature. The muscle groups in these joints are important not only in grasping the racket handle, but also in accommodating vibration upon contact with the ball. The musculatures involved are wrist flexor muscles and wrist extensor muscles. The wrist flexor muscles are located on the inside of the forearm. They run from the inside of the elbow to attach near the palm and fingers. The wrist extensor muscles are located on the outside of the forearm. These muscles run from the outside of the elbow and insert into the back of the hand and fingers. These two groups of muscles work together to coordinate grasping strength and to act as shock absorbers from vibration created from ball to racket contact. The wrist extensor muscles and tendons primarily absorb vibration at contact during a backhand stroke. More vibration is absorbed using a 1-handed backhand, as opposed to a 2-handed backhand. Conversely, the wrist flexor muscle tendons absorb vibration during forehand strokes.

These tissues are also a location of a common tennis related ailment.

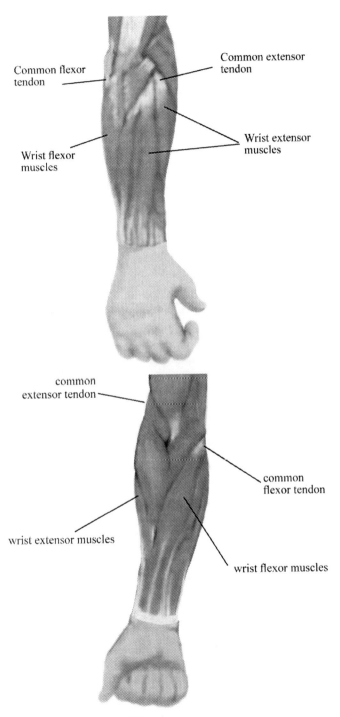

Elbow anatomy

2 common possible injuries exist:

- Lateral epicondylitis or "tennis elbow" is the most common. This is the inflammation or irritation of the wrist extensor muscle tendon near the outside of the elbow. This is characterized by pain along the outer edge of the elbow, weakness with grasping, and limited ability to perform repetitive activities such as grasping, hammering, or twisting. This often develops because of excessive repetitive vibration along this tendon beyond which it can reasonably tolerate.

- Medial epicondylitis or "golfer's elbow" is less common. This is the inflammation or irritation of the wrist flexor muscle tendons along the inside aspect of the elbow. It is characterized by similar limitations and weaknesses as tennis elbow, but the pain is along the inside of the elbow.

These injuries may be due to:

- muscle endurance weakness which prevents muscles from adequately handling vibration stress;

- a grip that is too tight which creates excessive force on these muscles and tendons;

- improper grip fit especially too small of a grip size;

- poor stroke technique such as making contact on groundstrokes (forehands and backhands) behind the body instead of slightly out in front;

- an overly heavy racket which requires more muscle effort to control;

- excessive string tension which translates more vibration to be absorbed into the forearm muscles.

Suggestions in reducing stress to these injured tissues are:

- Ensure that grip is of proper size. Tennis pro shops and stores are able to fit grips properly according to grip size.

- Play with a lighter weight racket.

- Use a racket with mid to oversized head for larger sweet spot to decrease vibration.

- Reduce string tension to 52-55 pounds to decrease vibration.

- Seek advice from a tennis professional for proper stroke mechanics and techniques.

- Utilize a strap just below the elbow to reduce stress on inflamed tendon.

<u>Prevention and rehabilitation considerations</u>: stretching and strengthening wrist flexors and extensors.

Goals for elbow and wrist stretching:
To achieve adequate flexibility and prevent tightness in wrist flexor and extensor muscles, which can lead to tennis elbow and wrist injuries. Please refer to stretching guidelines.

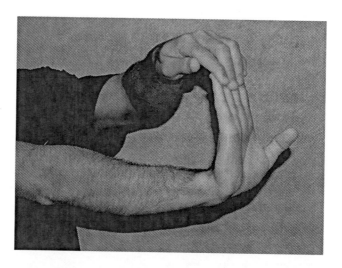

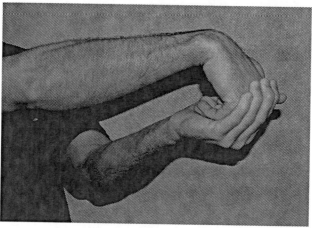

1. Wrist flexor stretch: stretches the wrist flexing muscles along the inside of the forearm. Extend arm to be stretched forward with palm up. Grasp fingers and hand with opposite hand and pull downward until mild stretch felt.

2. Wrist extensor stretch: stretches the wrist extending muscles along the outside of the forearm. Extend arm to be stretched forward with palm down. Grasp fingers and hand with opposite hand and pull downward until mild stretch is felt.

Goals for elbow and wrist strengthening: To properly condition wrist flexor and extensor muscles so that they may tolerate stresses involved with gripping and shock absorption of ball to racket contact. Please refer to strengthening guidelines.

1. Wrist flexion strengthening: strengthens the wrist flexing muscles along the inside of the forearm. Rest forearm on a surface with palm up, letting wrist and hand hang over the edge. Lift hand upward, keeping forearm stable. Return to starting position.

2. Wrist extension strengthening: strengthens the wrist extending muscles along the outside of the forearm. Rest forearm on a surface with palm down, letting wrist and hand hang over the edge. Lift hand upward, keeping forearm stable. Return to starting position.

3. Reverse bicep curl: strengthens elbow flexing and wrist extending muscles. Grasp free weight with palms downward. Keeping elbow stable at side, lift up on resistance by bending at elbows. Lift to full elbow bending then return to starting position.

4. Bar rolling: strengthens wrist flexing and extending muscles. Attach rope to center of a bar with weight on end of rope. Hold at each end of the bar with palms down. Roll bar forward to wind rope over bar until weight reaches bar. Then roll bar to unwind rope. This can be repeated rolling up backward. Also, bar rolling can be performed with palms facing upward.

THE SPINE

The spine is, without a doubt, the most important area of the body, not only in tennis related activity, but also in general everyday functioning. In many cases, it is also the most overlooked area of the body regarding training. The spine provides a stable core to the body for all activities and all uses of the arms and legs. Without proper spinal stability and health, it is much more difficult and possibly painful to adequately perform the activities and produce forces needed for tennis.

The spine is composed of 25 bones called vertebrae, which move on each other to produce motion through the spine. They run from the base of the head down to the tailbone. Each vertebra is separated by shock absorbing discs. The core of the body is stabilized by many muscles that surround the spine. The paraspinal muscles run along either side of the back of the spine. The spine also has smaller intrinsic or deep muscles that attach from one vertebra to the next. Along the front and side of the body are the abdominals and transverse obliques. Together these muscles not only produce forceful motions such as twisting, rotation, and bending, but also work in sync to provide a muscle "corset" to hold the spine in proper stable positions during activity. By holding the spine in these proper positions, the joints connecting one vertebra to the next and the discs between each vertebra are protected. When the muscles that protect and stabilize the spine are not well conditioned or flexible as possible, there is potential for injury.

Spine anatomy

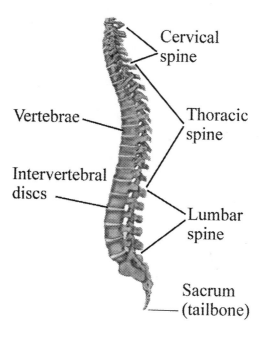

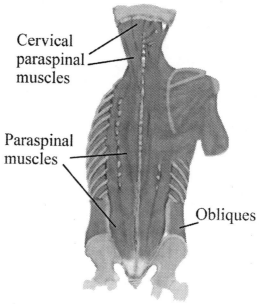

Common spine related issues are as follows:

- Muscle strains. These are small tears in the fibers that make up the muscle. This is usually characterized by a sudden "pulling" type of pain with activity. This results in pain with forward bending and lifting, as well as stiffness with back motion. These strains can involve both back and neck muscles or abdominal muscles.

    <u>Prevention and rehabilitation considerations</u>: stretch hamstring muscles and lower back muscles, and strengthen spinal muscles and core spine muscles. Examples: hamstring stretching, alternating arms/legs lying on stomach, seated flexion stretch.

- Spinal joint sprains or disc related injuries. These are small tears or disruptions in the tissues holding the vertebrae together or in the discs between the vertebrae. This may be associated with a sudden onset of injury, but are more likely caused by overuse types of problems. These problems may cause pain and stiffness at specific locations of the neck or back with certain neck and head movements and certain lower back movements. Neck and lower back turning or twisting and forward bending may be the most painful. More severe instances of these injuries could result in pain traveling down the arms or legs. This is due to irritation of spinal nerves that travel very close to the injured joint or disc.

    <u>Prevention and rehabilitation considerations</u>: improve lower back mobility with rotations and extension, stretch hamstrings and lower back muscles and strengthen core spinal muscles. Examples: lower trunk rotations, press ups on stomach, hamstring stretching while lying on back, bridging.

POSTURE

Another important rehabilitation and injury prevention consideration regarding the spine is posture. Optimally the spine is most healthy and effective when maintaining the normal curves as illustrated on page 32. A common problem today is the slouched posture. This posture develops from prolonged periods of slouching and stooping; for example working on computers or deskwork for long periods. Components of a slouched posture are: head leaning forward, shoulders rounded forward, rounded upper back and palms facing backwards in standing. These deviations are caused by tightness in the front of the neck and the chest, and weakness in the upper and lower back muscles and abdominals. When participating in increased physical activity with faulty spinal postures, it places abnormal stresses along the spinal muscles, joints throughout the spine and the discs in between the vertebrae. Over time these repetitive abnormal forces can create muscle strains and disc related injuries, such as disc herniations or ruptures. Thus, it is important to become aware of your posture and practice maintaining a more normal posture by keeping your shoulders back, head up and stomach tightened. This can be applied at any time, especially when sitting for prolonged periods. The more you practice this the more automatic this posture will become for you in all situations.

Goals for spine stretching: To achieve adequate flexibility through spinal and abdominal muscles and joints to allow for full spine motion in tennis play. Please refer to stretching guidelines.

1. Neck side bending stretch: stretches the upper trapezius neck muscles. Reach hand over opposite side of head and pull head toward shoulder until mild stretch is felt.

2. Neck side bending stretch variation: stretches the levator scapula neck muscles. Reach hand over opposite side of head and pull head in front of shoulder until mild stretch is felt.

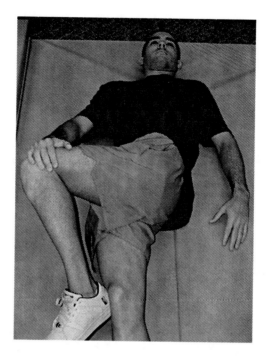

3. Back rotation stretch: stretches lower back muscles. Lying on back, lift knee up and pull with opposite arm across body. Maintain both shoulders flat on surface.

4. Back flexion stretch: stretches lower back muscles. Seated in chair, lean trunk forward between legs while providing light pull with hands on ankles.

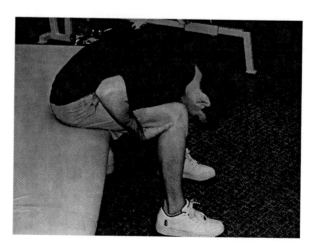

 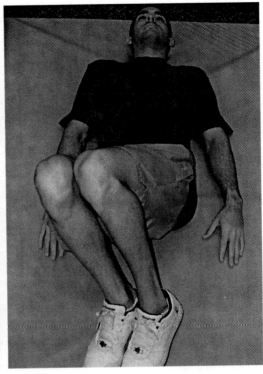

5. Back extension stretch- stretches abdominals and lower back joints. While standing, place both hands on the back of hips. Lean backward while supporting movement with hands on hips.

6. Lower trunk rotation- effective with lower back injuries. This will help to stretch lower back musculature and lower back joints. Lying on back with both knees bent up, rotate both knees to one side as far as comfortable, then rotate back to other side.

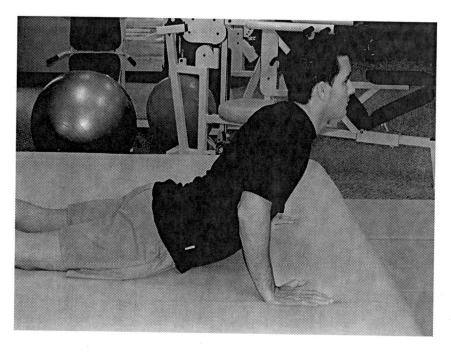

7. Lying back extension- Effective with lower back injuries. Stretches abdominals and lower back joints. Lie on stomach. Place hands in a push up position. Extend arms to raise shoulders off of floor, but keeping hips on floor.

<u>Goals for spine strengthening</u>: VERY IMPORTANT! To properly condition, strengthen and stabilize spine related core tissues and musculature to produce more power with tennis stroke performance, as well as to maintain healthy spinal positions/postures. Maintaining this strong stabilized core will prevent injury and allow for better execution of all extremities during tennis and also general everyday activity. Please refer to stretching guidelines.

1a. Plank shown on knees and feet: strengthens abdominal muscles and lower back stabilizing muscles. Lie on stomach. Prop up onto elbows and knees while maintaining a straight spine or "plank" position. Hold for 3-5 seconds then relax.

1b. Progression: Lie on stomach, but prop up onto elbows and feet, maintaining straight legs and spine. Increasing the duration of the hold to 10 seconds will also progress strengthening.

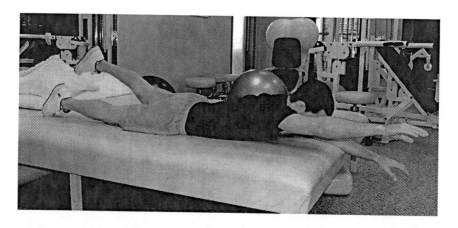

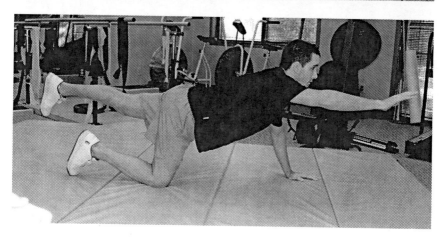

2a. Alternating arm and leg on stomach: strengthens back musculature. Lie on stomach with arms out in front. Raise one arm and opposite leg about 4-6 inches off of floor, then return down and perform on other arm and opposite leg.

2b. Progression. Alternating arm and leg on ball: strengthens back muscles and includes strengthening of lower back stabilizing muscles. Lie over exercise ball with both hands and feet on floor. Perform alternating arm and opposite leg, while maintaining a steady position on ball. Key is to minimize trunk movement on ball while alternating arm and leg.

2c. Progression. Alternating arm and leg on all fours: strengthens back muscles and includes strengthening of lower back stabilizing muscles. Achieve an "all fours" position on hands and knees. Alternate raising one arm and straighten opposite leg while maintaining steady "all fours" position.

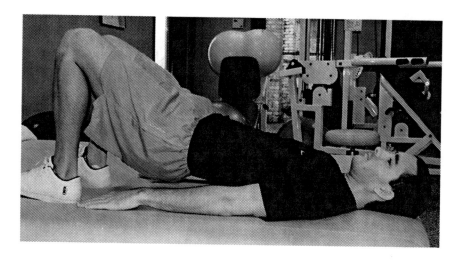

3a. Bridging: strengthens lower back musculature. Lie on back with both knees bent. Push through feet to raise buttocks off the floor about 8 inches while maintaining a straight spine. Return down.

3b. Progression. Bridging on ball: strengthens lower back muscles and stabilizers. Lie on back with feet resting on exercise ball and slight bend in knees. Push through feet on ball to raise buttocks off the floor about 8 inches, while maintain straight spine and preventing exercise ball from moving.

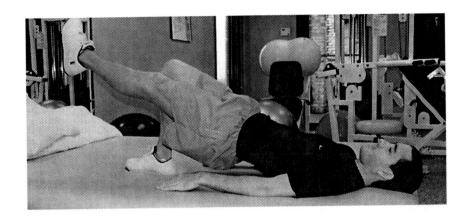

4a. Progression. Alternating legs with bridging: strengthens lower back muscles and is a very good strengthening activity for deep lower back stabilizing muscles. Lie on back with knees bent. Push through feet to raise buttocks off the floor about 6-8 inches. Maintain straight spine and elevated buttocks while alternating raising legs off the floor.

4b. Progression. Alternating legs with bridging on ball: strengthens lower back muscles and is a very good strengthening activity for deep lower back stabilizing muscles. Lie on back with feet resting on exercise ball and knees slightly bent. Push through feet on ball to raise buttocks off the floor about 6-8 inches. Maintain straight spine and elevated buttocks while alternating raising legs off the exercise ball.

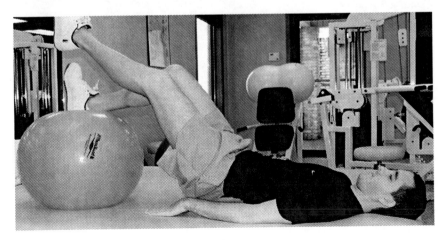

5. Marching lying over ball: strengthens spine stabilizing muscles. Lie on back over ball with ball under mid to upper back area. Maintain straight spine and stable exercise ball while alternating raising knees up.

6. Pelvic tilts-effective with lower back injuries. Provides strengthening to abdominals and mild stretching of lower back joints. Lie on back with both knees bent. Rotate hips backward until lower back is pushing into the floor. Do not raise buttocks off of floor. Hold position 2-3 seconds then relax.

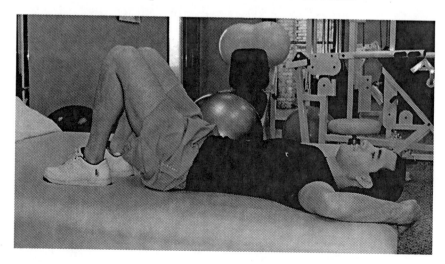

THE HIP AND KNEE

The hip and knee are important weight bearing joints in propelling a tennis player around the court. Weight bearing joints refer to those that support the weight of the body during movement. Good court mobility requires the hip and knee to be able to produce quick accelerations, decelerations, sprints and frequent forceful changes of direction. Thus, over the course of a match, these joints endure much stress through forceful muscle activity, wide ranges of joint motion and tolerating the repetitive leg to ground impact.

The hip is quite similar to the shoulder in that it is a very mobile or flexible joint, but in turn sacrifices some stability. Like the shoulder, it relies upon muscle strength for added stability. The knee is not as mobile as the hip, but may be more important in carrying out forces necessary to create desired movement. These two joints share many common structures which aid in force production during mobility. Along the front of the hip and knee are the quadriceps muscles. These are the large muscles of the upper thigh that allow straightening of the knee, performing squatting types of activities and propelling one forward. In the back of the leg and knee are the hamstrings. The hamstrings are not considered to be as important as the quadriceps by many athletes, but in actuality are just as important. The hamstrings are essential in propelling one in a certain direction as well as helping to stabilize the knee during these quick and forceful

Hip and Knee Anatomy

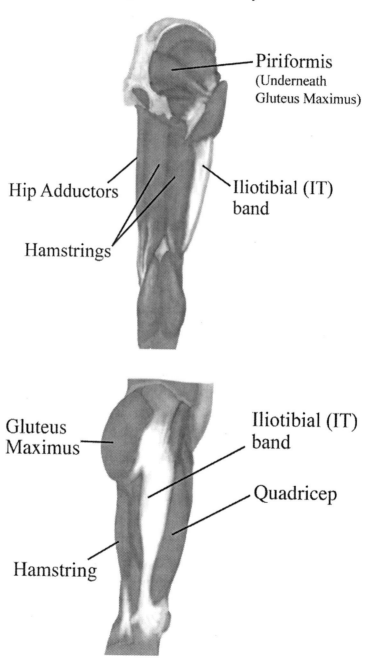

motions. Therefore, it is very important that the hamstrings be nearly as strong and properly conditioned as the quadriceps. Along the inside of the thigh and hip are the hip adductors or groin muscles. These muscles serve to stabilize the hip and assist in changing direction. Another important muscle involving the hip is the piriformis muscle. This muscle is located in the back of the hip and somewhat acts as the "rotator cuff" of the hip by assisting in stability. This muscle undergoes forceful contractions over the course of tennis play and may tend to develop excessive tightness. When this muscle becomes less flexible, it can affect the performance of the hip as well as significantly affect the position and health of the spine.

Another important tissue involving the hip and knee is the iliotibial band or IT band. This is a rather thick tendonous band, which runs from the outside of the hip down to the outside of the knee. This band helps to provide stability to both the hip and knee. If this tendonous band becomes too tight, which is common with running and sprinting types of activities, it can cause increased friction along the outside of the hip and possibly abnormal tension on the knee cap. This abnormal tension can prevent the kneecap from gliding properly and result in irritation to the under side of the kneecap.

Given that the hip and knee require large ranges of motion to participate in tennis, flexibility is a big part of these joints. The quadriceps, hamstrings, hip adductors and IT band need to be flexible enough to allow the hip and knee joints to move through their full available range of motion. If flexibility is not adequate, excessive stress may be placed on the muscles as they contract, thus causing potential for muscle strains.

Having adequate hip and knee flexibility is also extremely important in maintaining proper lower back health. When these muscles are tight they tend to pull abnormally on the hip bones, which in turn can place the lower back joints and musculature in poor postures. This can predispose for lower back injury.

By virtue of the hip and knee joints being weight bearing joints during rigorous activity, their joint surfaces or cartilage are subjected to compression and friction forces through leg to ground contact. Over time, the repetitive exposure to these forces during tennis play can potentially create a breakdown of this protective joint cartilage and development of arthritis in these joints can result. Since the primary job of this cartilage is to provide stability and cushioning in the knee and hip, arthritis or breakdown of this cartilage may significantly limit hip and knee function through pain and instability. By maintaining adequate muscle strength and conditioning and joint flexibility, the risk of developing this cartilage deterioration is lessened.

Common hip and knee related injuries are:

- Muscle strains of the hamstrings, quadriceps and hip adductors: These are small tears within the muscle fibers caused by excessive muscle force production over a stretched muscle. This is characterized by a sudden "pulling" sensation in the quadriceps or hamstring and results in painful and tightness with walking, running, or squatting. More severe instances can have swelling and bruising.

    <u>Prevention and rehabilitation considerations</u>: stretch and strengthen hamstrings, groin and quadriceps muscles.

- Cartilage or meniscal tears in the knee: This is a disruption or tearing of protective cartilage or meniscus in the knee. This can be sudden in onset or gradual over time. This will cause pain along the knee joint with straightening, bending and twisting of the knee, especially when weight bearing/standing. Motion in the knee will also be limited. More severe tears can include swelling and a clicking, popping, or catching sensation in the knee with movement.

<u>Prevention and rehabilitation considerations</u>: stretch and strengthen hamstrings and quadriceps and maintain or improve knee motion to a full range; reduce and prevent swelling in knee. Examples: hamstring and quadriceps stretching, seated knee curls, leg press; knee sleeve to provide extra stability and reduce swelling.

- Tendonitis in the knee: This is irritation of the patellar tendon which connects the kneecap to the lower leg bone (tibia). This injury is due to gradual overuse and overstressing of this tendon by overworking a less than adequately conditioned tendon and quadriceps muscle or due to chronic tightness in the hamstring muscle. It is characterized by pain below the kneecap when running, squatting, and going up stairs. More severe instances may involve swelling just below the kneecap.

<u>Prevention and rehabilitation considerations</u>: stretch and strengthen hamstrings and quadriceps; reduce stress on patellar tendon by using patellar strap.

- Knee ligament sprains: This is usually associated with a sudden onset of injury. Commonly sprained ligaments in the knee are the MCL (medial collateral ligament) and ACL (anterior cruciate ligament). These injuries are often a result of excessive side bending or twisting of the knee while the leg is planted on the ground. This places more stress on the ligaments than they can accommodate, thus contributing to a small to large tear. This is characterized by instant knee pain, limitation in knee motion, and weakness in the knee. Swelling may also be present. Because these ligaments are critical to knee stability, these injuries require avoiding tennis play for a period of time depending on the severity.

<u>Prevention and rehabilitation considerations</u>: strengthen hamstrings and quadriceps together to promote stability, maintain or improve knee motion, prevent or reduce swelling. Examples: leg press, small range squatting or lunges and utilizing knee sleeve to improve stability and reduce swelling. A more aggressive rigid knee brace may be necessary if the ligament sprain is more severe.

- Hip and knee arthritis: This is the gradual wearing down of the hip and knee protective cartilage over time. It is caused by repetitive forceful impact of the legs on hard surfaces, such as required in tennis. This is characterized by gradual increase in aching pains in the hip or knee, limitation with hip and knee flexibility, pain with squatting and stairs, and increased stiffness and aching in the mornings. Changing court surfaces from hard to softer surfaces (i.e. clay or grass) will help reduce force of impact, thus reduce stress on this protective cartilage.

<u>Prevention and rehabilitation considerations</u>: improve motion in hip and knee through stretching; stretch piriformis, hamstrings, quadriceps and groins muscles; reduce court impact. Examples: piriformis, hamstring, groin, quadriceps stretches; play on a softer court (clay) to lessen impact on joints; utilize knee sleeve to reduce swelling.

- Patellofemoral syndrome: This is the wearing down of the cartilage on the underside of the kneecap, due to improper gliding along the front of the knee during contracting of the quadriceps. The improper gliding is affected by tightness in the IT band and weakness in the quadriceps. Abnormal hip or foot/ankle postures can also contribute to this condition. This is characterized by pain and/or swelling around the kneecap or on the tendon below the kneecap. Painful activities include squatting, running, and stairs.

Prevention and rehabilitation considerations: improve IT band flexibility and strengthen quadriceps and hips. Shoe modification may be required if abnormal foot/ankle postures are present (this will be discussed further in the following chapter). Utilization of varying taping methods and knee sleeves may be effective in assisting with correcting kneecap gliding.

Goals for hip and knee stretching: To achieve optimal flexibility in quadriceps, hamstrings, piriformis and IT bands. This will allow for unhindered hip and knee mobility. Please refer to stretching guidelines.

1. Standing hamstring stretch: Stretches the hamstrings along the back of the upper leg. Place leg to be stretched on raised surface with knee straight. Bend trunk forward over that knee keeping knee straight. Repeat with other leg. **Caution: this stretch may not be appropriate for those with a history of lower back pain.**

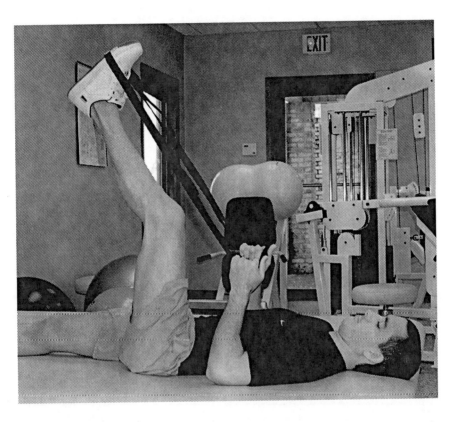

2. Hamstring stretch lying on back: <u>Effective hamstring stretch for those with history of lower back pain.</u> Lie on back. Bring knee up until upper leg is perpendicular to floor and other leg resting straight on floor. Using rope, towel, etc. pull raised foot upward until moderate stretch is felt behind upper leg. Repeat with other leg.

3. Standing quadriceps stretch: Stretches quadriceps muscles along front of thigh. Using one hand for balance and other to pull upward on foot, pull foot toward buttocks while keeping that knee directly under hips until stretch is felt along front of thigh. Repeat with other leg.

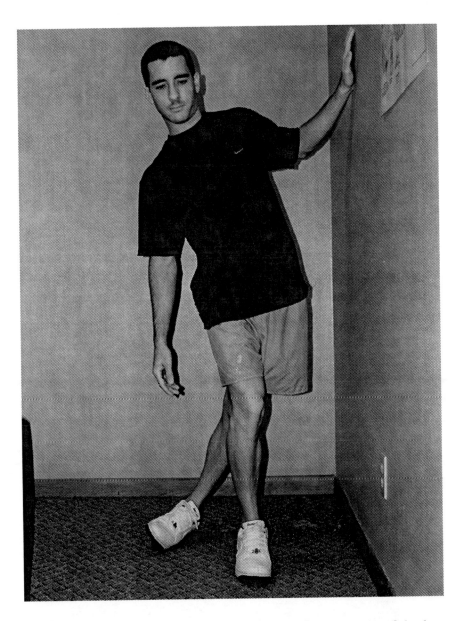

4. IT band stretch: Stretches IT band along the outside of the hip and thigh. Stand with leg to be stretched on side of wall. Cross opposite leg in front of leg to be stretched. Lean hip toward wall and shoulders away from wall until stretch is felt along outside of hip and upper leg.

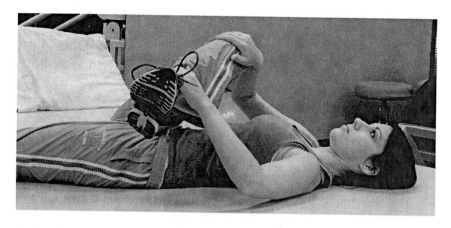

5. Piriformis stretch: Stretches piriformis muscle deep within buttocks. Lying on back, pull one knee towards chest and opposite shoulder. At the same time with other hand pull ankle towards shoulder. Stretch should be felt in back of hips.

6. Groin stretch: Stretches the adductor muscles along the inner thighs. Sit with bottoms of both feet pulled together with knees flexed. Provide downward push on knees using hands to elicit stretch.

Goals for hip and knee strengthening: to properly condition quadriceps, hamstrings and piriformis. This will improve tolerance to tennis activity. Also, strengthening will help to stabilize the hip and knee joints to allow for better stress accommodation from impact and to enhance joint performance. Please refer to strengthening guidelines.

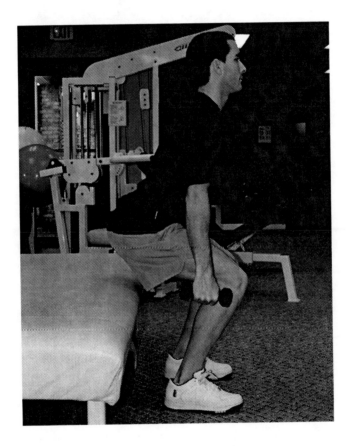

1. Squatting: Primarily strengthens quadriceps and gluteal muscles, along with hamstrings to lesser degree. Stand with feet shoulder width apart and slightly turned outward. Bend knees, thus lowering buttocks down and slightly back. **Ensure that knees remain behind front of feet to prevent excessive stress on the knees.** Chair may be placed behind to guide depth of squat. Additional resistance may be used with dumbbells.

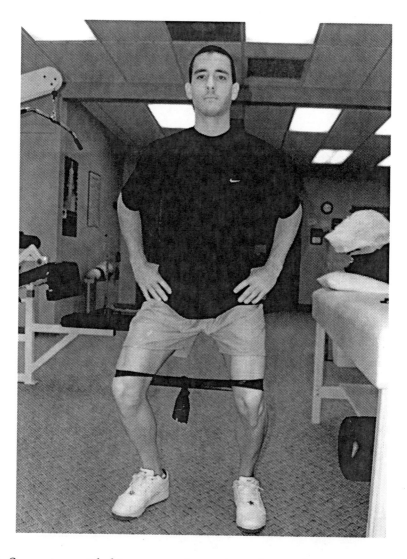

2. Squatting with hip external rotation: Strengthens quadriceps, gluteal muscles and piriformis muscles for better hip stabilization. Stand with feet shoulder width apart and elastic band with light tension around knees. Achieve and hold a slight squat position. Then rotate one leg outward against resistance of the elastic band. Repeat with other leg.

3. Alternating forward lunges: Strengthens quadriceps and gluteal muscles, along with hamstrings to lesser degree. Begin by standing with feet together. Step forward with one leg while lowering other knee toward floor. **<u>Remember to keep front of knee behind front of foot.</u>** Push back to return to standing. Alternate with other leg.

4. Lateral lunging-progression with elastic band: Strengthens hip abductor muscles along outer hip, as well as gluteal and quadriceps muscles. Stand with elastic band around knees with mild tension. Step sideways with one leg pulling against tension of elastic band while performing moderate squat. Continue to step in that direction for desired repetitions, and then repeat in direction of other leg.

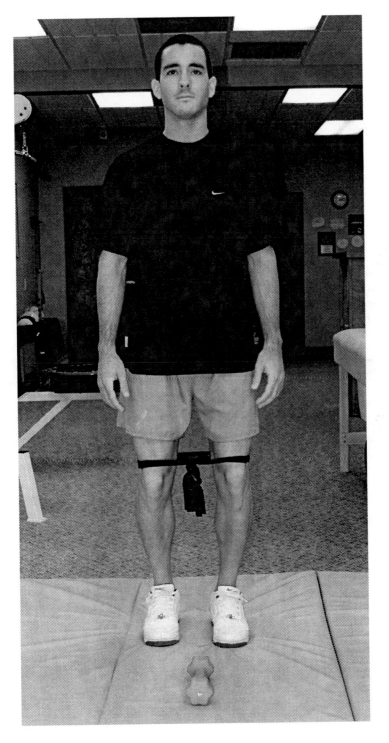

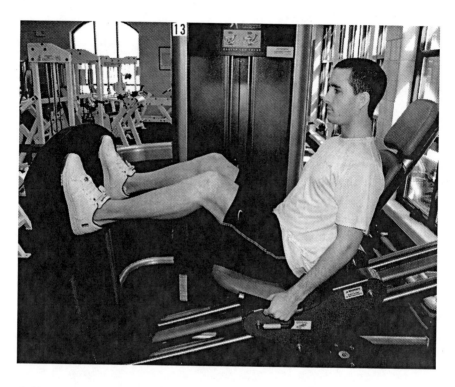

5. Leg press: Strengthens quadriceps and gluteal muscles. Sit on leg press machine with feet placed on platform shoulder width apart and turned slightly outward. Push through feet to slide seat backward and return slowly to starting position. <u>Feet height should be high enough to prevent knees from moving in front of feet.</u>

6. Seated knee flexion: Strengthens hamstring muscles along back of thighs. Seated on machine, align knee joint with pivot point of machine. Begin with knees straight. Pull back with both feet until knees are nearly fully flexed. Return slowly to starting position.

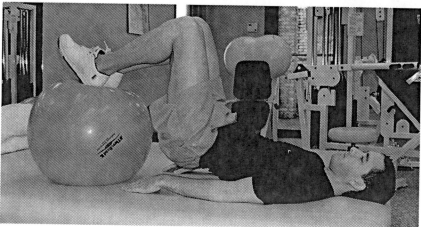

7. Knee flexion on ball: Strengthens hamstring muscles and lower back extensor muscles. Lie on back with feet over exercise ball. Push through feet to raise buttocks. Maintain raised buttocks for whole set. Pull ball toward trunk using feet, then return ball to starting position.

8. **Single legged ball squat:** Strengthens quadriceps and gluteal muscles, and improves balance strength in hips, knees and ankles. Begin with one foot placed on exercise ball. Squat with front knee while rolling ball back with other foot. Goal is to control ball while executing squat and maintaining balance. Then return to standing upright position by straightening leg and rolling ball back forwards. Switch legs once set is completed. If unable to adequately control ball during one legged squat, one can place foot on a stable surface such as a chair/bench to execute squat. When proficient at this a transition can be made to utilizing the ball.

THE FOOT AND ANKLE

The ankle is one of the most complex joints in our bodies and one of the most important in tennis. The interaction of many weight bearing joints and tissues within the foot and ankle contribute to proper mechanics in not only the foot and ankle, but also up into the knee, hip and lower back. Disruption in the foot and ankle mechanics can result in problems to these areas. The goals of the ankle are to assist with propelling the body in different directions, reduce shock absorption upon contact with the ground, and also to help the feet accommodate to different surfaces for improved balance.

The two main joints in the ankle are the talocrural joint and subtalar joint. The talocrural joint allows for pointing the foot up and down and helping with moving it side to side. It also aids in force production for propelling one in a given direction. The subtalar joint serves an equally important purpose. This joint is deeper in the ankle and into the mid foot area. It controls the finer intrinsic movements of the foot and ankle necessary to control and support the arches along the bottom of the foot. By doing this, it allows for the foot and ankle to accommodate to different surfaces, thus enabling for optimal balance and effective propulsion or force production essential in movement.

Foot and ankle stability is enhanced by various muscles and ligaments surrounding the ankle and along the bottom of the foot. The muscles which affect the ankle and foot are the gastronemius (calf muscle), located along the back of the lower leg and ankle; peroneal muscles, located along the outside of the lower leg and ankle; posterior tibialis, located along the inside of the lower leg and ankle; and anterior tibialis, located along the front of the lower leg and ankle. These muscles, along with other small muscles and ligaments that surround the ankle, work together to provide stability in every direction. It is this stability that is essential in tennis because of the frequent, quick changes in direction and movement that are required. Proper strengthening and conditioning of these muscles enhance their ability to stabilize the foot and ankle during vigorous tennis play.

Flexibility of the gastronemius or calf muscle is also very important. Given that this muscle undergoes much forceful repetitive contracting while playing tennis, it may tend to become tight. When tight, it can limit or prevent full necessary motion in the ankle, decrease strength and also put excessive stress on other ankle structures, which could place these structures in poor mechanical positions.

One such tissue affected by the gastrocnemius is the plantar fascia. The plantar fascia is a thick tendonous band which runs from the bottom of the heel to the base of the toes. Its function is to assist in supporting the arches along the bottom of the foot, especially during impact with the ground. During foot to ground impact with walking, jogging or running, forces will pull the foot's arch downward. It is the plantar fascia which helps to maintain this arch stability and disperse force created by foot to ground contact. By maintaining this stability it allows for effective and efficient production of forces by the legs to promote movement. Given the repetitive high impact nature of tennis, this plantar fascia undergoes much stress, which over time could lead to irritation. Also, when calf musculature is tight it will pull on the heel, which in turn places more stress through tension on the plantar fascia. This will further predispose for aggravation or injury to the plantar fascia.

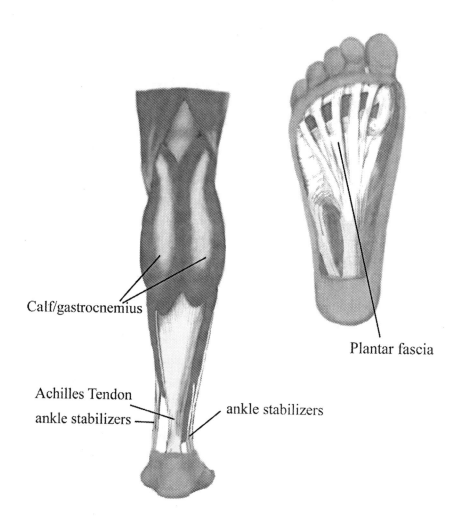

Another important factor to consider regarding foot and ankle health in tennis is posture. Since the foot and ankle have numerous joints and muscles that work together while weight bearing, it is fairly common for slight abnormalities in the posture or positioning of the foot and ankle to be present. In a normal standing position, the foot should be aligned pointing in a forward direction with a good arch. This good arch means that the middle of the bottom of the foot should be raised slightly off of the floor when standing. Common abnormalities in foot and ankle positions are over pronating and over supinating. Over pronating refers to the arch of the foot collapsing when standing, giving a "flat footed" appearance. This is usually due to excessive subtalar joint mobility or instability. Over supinating is when there is too much stiffness in the arch, thus demonstrating a high arch when standing.

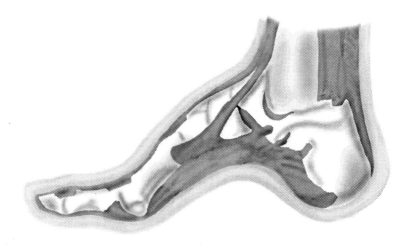

Oversupinated

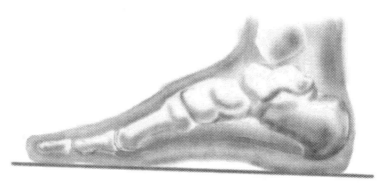

Neutral

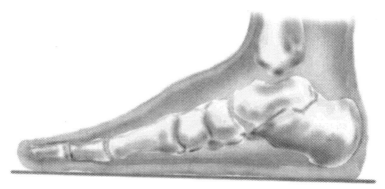

Overpronated

Differences such as these can contribute to limited tolerance of muscles, ligaments, and joints to tennis related activity. Proper ankle and foot strengthening and stretching can certainly improve this tolerance and even help with foot and ankle alignment, but in more severe instances shoe modification and orthotic intervention may be required. Wearing specifically designed tennis shoes may help with foot and ankle posture:

- Over pronating feet (flat footed) should have shoes with good arch support in the form of a ridge built into the inside of the sole. This helps to provide the arch with needed stability.

- Over supinating feet (high arches) are generally more stiff, thus requiring more cushioning in the sole of the shoe to help with shock absorption. Gel insoles may be effective to assist with cushioning.

Orthotics are more specifically designed for varying types of foot and ankle postures. Over the counter shoe inserts/orthotics are sometimes useful, but they are most effectively fitted by trained specialists, such as physical therapists, orthopedic doctors and podiatrists based upon thorough evaluations of the particular foot and ankle.

Other common foot and ankle related problems:

- Ankle sprains: this is the acute or sudden "rolling over" of the ankle when planting the foot to change direction. The foot usually rolls under the body, which causes small to larger tears in the ligament(s) or tendon(s) along the outside of the ankle. This may result in bruising and swelling, and usually requires rest from tennis play for a period of time.

<u>Prevention and rehabilitation considerations</u>: strengthen ankle eversion muscles and ankle stabilizing muscles. Examples: resisted ankle eversion with elastic band and single leg standing ball tossing.

- Gastrocnemius (calf) strains: these are small tears within the muscle fibers of the calf due to excessive force production by this muscle. This may result in swelling and painful walking.

  <u>Prevention and rehabilitation considerations</u>: stretch calf muscles and tendons. Example: standing calf stretch.

- Achilles tendonitis: this is the inflammation or irritation of the thick tendon connecting the calf muscle to the heel. This injury is more related to overuse and will gradually increase over time. It is characterized by pain behind the heel and tightness in this area when getting out of bed in the morning and with walking. Swelling may also be noted in this area. This tendonitis is commonly associated with calf tightness and plantar fascia pain.

  <u>Prevention and rehabilitation considerations</u>: stretch calf muscles and tendons, and plantar fascia along bottom of foot. Examples: standing calf stretch, standing plantar fascia stretch, and plantar fascia ball stretch.

- Shin splints: this is inflammation of muscles along the front, inside, or outside of the lower leg which assist with ankle motion and subtalar (arch) control. This is characterized by pain along the shin bone (tibia) with activity. It usually subsides with rest. It may be caused by poor arch stability or inappropriate footwear.

  <u>Prevention and rehabilitation considerations</u>: strengthen ankle inversion muscles and consider more appropriate footwear or arch support depending on foot type. Examples: resisted ankle

inversions with elastic band; possible need for additional arch support.

- Plantarfasciitis: this is the inflammation of the plantar fascia due to repetitive over-stretching. This is characterized by pain along the bottom of the foot and near the heel. Pain increases with walking and running activities, and is often tight upon getting out of bed in the morning. This can be associated with excessive calf and Achilles tendon tightness, poor footwear or faulty foot and ankle posture.

    <u>Prevention and rehabilitation considerations</u>: stretch calf muscles and tendons, and plantar fascia along bottom of foot; consider more appropriate footwear or arch support. Examples: standing calf stretch, standing plantar fascia stretch, and plantar fascia ball stretch; possible need for additional arch support.

- Pain or callous formation on or around the toes: This is a result of repetitive friction on the toes from footwear during frequent forceful stopping and accelerating movements. Bruising to toes and toenail damage may also evident. This may be worsened by poor fitting footwear.

    <u>Prevention and rehabilitation considerations</u>: consider more appropriate footwear. Generally wearing a half size larger may assist in decreasing friction on toes by allowing more room for movement. Wearing an extra pair of socks may help with cushioning. Also, changing socks during play regularly if sweat accumulation becomes excessive will help prevent friction.

<u>Goals for foot and ankle stretching</u>: to gain full flexibility of gastronemius/calf muscle. This will allow for full ankle motion. Also, stretching will prevent tightness in plantar fascia. This commonly occurs with tennis participation. Please refer to stretching guidelines.

1. Calf/heel cord stretch: stretches muscle and tendon along back of lower leg and heel. Stand with leg to be stretched back and other leg forward. Place rear foot flat and pointing forward. Lean hips forward, maintaining rear foot flat and knee straight. Stretch will be felt along calf.

2. Plantar fascia stretch in corner: stretches tissue along bottom of feet. Stand with foot to be stretched across corner of floor and wall. Lean hips forward. Stretch will be felt behind ankle, along bottom of foot and in calf.

3. Plantar fascia stretch using tennis ball: stretches and massages tissue along bottom of feet. While sitting place tennis ball under bare foot. Push down on that knee to increase pressure onto ball while rolling foot backward and forward over the ball.

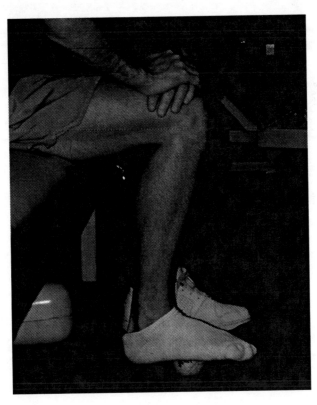

Goals for foot and ankle strengthening: to properly strengthen all ankle and foot musculature to ensure optimal stability for improved tolerance to demands of tennis participation. Please refer to strengthening guidelines.

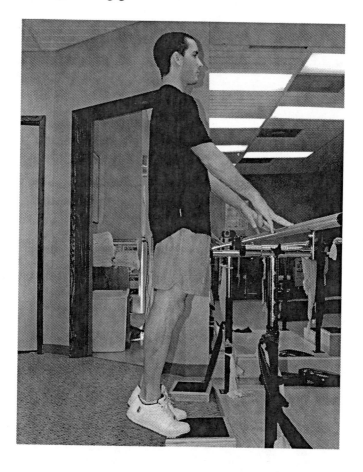

1a. Heel raises: strengthens calf muscle and tendons. Standing with feet apart at a normal stance width, push with front of feet to elevate heels off of floor. Return to starting position. For progression: stand on the edge of a step to allow heels to return further downward; utilize dumbbells for extra resistance. Also, by not using hands to assist with balance, ankle coordination and stabilization strength will be addressed.

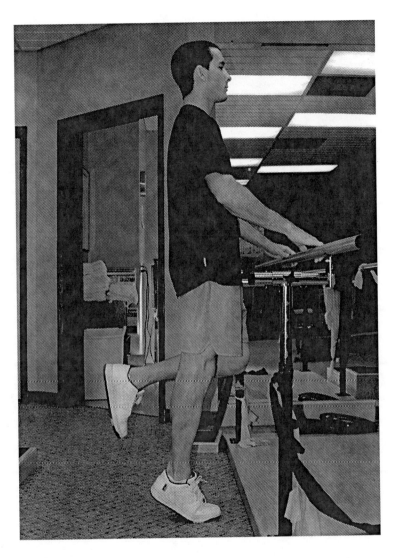

1b. Progression- single legged heel raises: Strengthens calf muscle and tendon, as well as ankle stabilizers. Stand on one leg. Push with front of foot to elevate heel off of floor. For progression: stand on the edge of a step to allow heels to return further downward; utilize dumbbells for extra resistance. Also, by avoiding the use of the hands to assist with balance, ankle coordination and stabilization strength will be further addressed.

3. Single legged standing balance-dynamic: strengthens ankle stabilizing muscles for better coordination and balance. Stand on one leg and perform arm movements to challenge balance. Such movements may include ball tossing, arm raises, elastic band pulling. Goal is to maintain balance on one foot for up to 30 seconds. Repeat other leg.

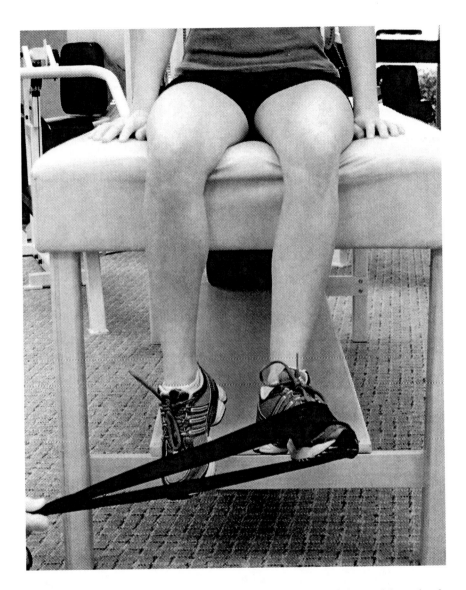

4. Resisted ankle eversion: strengthens outside of the ankle, which helps prevent ankle sprains. Seated with elastic band looped around front of foot pulling inwards. With foot only, rotate foot outward against resistance. Repeat other ankle.

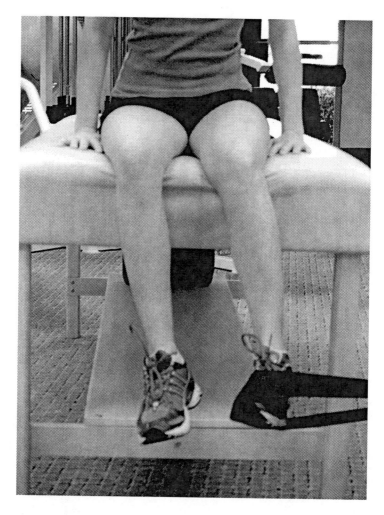

5. Resisted ankle inversion: Effective for flat feet postures. Strengthens arch supporting muscles, which will assist with arch stability. Seated with elastic band looped around front of foot pulling outward. With foot only, rotate foot inwards and up against resistance. Repeat other ankle.

INJURY IDENTIFICATION

An important aspect to consider when playing tennis regularly is determining when body discomfort is just typical muscle soreness or indication of a more serious problem. It is very common and likely that one experiences a degree of soreness possibly during and after playing tennis; however, there is a point where lingering soreness can suggest a problem. While playing tennis, it is normal to experience a degree of muscle fatigue, which also may contribute to soreness. This may be due to the depletion of electrolytes within the body (sodium and potassium to name two) or the accumulation of lactic acid. When this soreness is in conjunction with pain moving through full motion in a joint or notable weakness when performing a stroke or moving about the court, it may be an indication of a developing problem. A good general rule of thumb to keep in mind is that typical muscle and joint soreness can and may last up to 24 to 48 hours. This is referred to as delayed onset muscle soreness (DOMS). Within this time frame, one should begin to notice a decrease (if not full recovery) of this soreness. If this soreness persists for longer than 48 hours accompanied by weakness and difficulty moving joints through a full motion, this may be a potential injury. These injuries will gradually progress over time with cumulative stress. These injuries are the overuse injuries. With overuse injuries, tissue breakdown or damage will have begun before pain is perceived. It may begin with subtle soreness and/or pain, and possibly joint stiffness. These symptoms may subside and tennis play will continue, because pain is not limiting. However, these symptoms (soreness, pain, stiffness) will persist with tennis activity and increase over time until significant limitation with performance is experienced. When this significant pain and limitation develops, more severe tissue breakdown has occurred. These situations often call for extended periods away from tennis and possibly additional medical treatment. It is important that early recognition of overuse injuries is achieved. By recognizing early signs of progressing soreness and stiffness, proper attention can be given to these tissues to address the problem before much more significant damage is done. A common example of this is lateral epicondylitis or tennis elbow. This injury often begins as mild soreness along the outside of the dominant elbow, but with repeated participation in stressful activity will soon progress to severe inflammation. Once at this point, cessation of tennis play may be necessary for up to 6 weeks or longer.

If this scenario happens after each session of tennis play and with worsening pain, weakness, stiffness, or continually prolonged recovery times, it may be wise to seek the advice of an orthopedic physician. Regarding the safety of return to tennis participation, it is good to employ this strategy in order to avoid over stressing of susceptible tissues. <u>One should have fully recovered from their prior tennis play before setting foot on the court again.</u> If a particular tissue is still irritated or recovering from a prior match and is subjected to stress and exertion again, further tissue aggravation is certain.

There are the more obvious injuries associated with tennis, the acute injuries. These injuries are the sprains, strains or even fractures. They happen in one specific onset and are very noticeable when they occur. They are characterized by immediate pain and limited function or stability in a muscle or joint. This may require immediate stopping of play depending on the severity of the injury. More serious injuries which may significantly limit not only tennis participation, but daily functioning should be evaluated by a physician. Again, it is important to allow these tissues full recovery time before resuming tennis play.

Other factors which may effect tennis health and contribute to injury:

- Age is certainly a factor when dealing with health of joints and muscles during tennis play. Both younger and older individuals have factors to consider. With children and teenagers growth spurts are inevitable. Some go through gradual spurts, and others are more dramatic. During these growth spurts bones may grow at a faster rate than what the muscles and tendons can accept. This can lead to development of muscle tightness and possibly weakness. In this situation it is important to maintain stretching while these muscles and tendons catch up to the new length of the bones.

  As we all age our bodies have gradually less ability to repair themselves rapidly. About the age of 27-30 our bodies will start to heal a little less rapidly; thus over time our bodies will not recover as quickly regarding physical activity. Also, over time the protective cartilage in our joints and shock absorbing discs in our spine will lose some thickness. This is most prevalent in weight bearing joints such as knees, hips and in the lower spine. By losing this thickness our joints have less cushioning to absorb the foot to ground impact in tennis. This is why playing on a softer surface (clay or grass) is better for these weight bearing joints. Muscles also may become less flexible with age. This contributes to abnormal joint motion and can predispose for joint injuries and protective cartilage breakdown. Maintaining a regular stretching routine is essential.

- Another factor to consider is technique. Proper techniques not only allow for more efficient strokes, but also enable muscles and joints to work in a correct mechanical pattern. By these muscles and joints working correctly over many repetitions, it prevents overstressing of these tissues. This will significantly reduce the "wear and tear" to these structures. If faulty mechanics or techniques continue, then tissues will be subjected to overuse and overstress. This can predispose for degenerative problems within joints or tendonitis. Consulting with a tennis professional is encouraged to evaluate and address any mechanical problems.

- Pregnancy is also a very important consideration for women. Activity is usually encouraged during the first two trimesters of pregnancy and tennis is a good outlet for fitness. The problem is that during pregnancy a woman's body begins to produce a hormone called relaxin. This hormone prepares the body for childbirth by loosening or "relaxing" ligaments. This is most necessary for the pelvic girdle; however it may also tend to relax other ligaments throughout the body. These loosened ligaments are now providing less stability in the joints they surround; thus, joints may not be strong enough to handle the full rigors of tennis. By preventing very aggressive movement around the court and powerful strokes, it should protect these temporarily loosened joints from injury.

WHEN INJURIES OCCUR

When an injury is suspected or has occurred there are several measures to take depending on the severity of the injury. These measures range from treating the acute situation to modifications for continuing tennis play.

Treating the acute injury: This injury occurs with one traumatic event. (Examples: ankle sprains, muscle strains): Upon first detecting an injury, it is important to reduce pain, inflammation and swelling in the involved body part. These factors will impede the healing process of the injured tissues. Reducing these factors will allow the body to heal itself more efficiently.

- First, aggravation of the injured tissue should be prevented. This is accomplished by avoiding activities, which cause increased pain and swelling to the injured area. These activities will place excessive stress on injured tissues, which are unable to tolerate this stress. This will contribute to further tissue irritation and possibly injury.

- Secondly, reduction of tissue swelling is done by utilizing ice and elevating the involved area. Ice is effective in decreasing localized blood flow, which decreases fluids that contribute to swelling. Applying ice to the injured area is most effective for 10 minutes. Longer durations may decrease the benefit and possibly contribute to tissue death or frost bite. Elevation utilizes the effects of gravity to assist in reduction of swelling.

- Light compression in the form of an elastic wrap is also beneficial in reducing localized swelling.

After the injury begins to heal and less pain is experienced, it is important to initiate a gradual progressive return to tennis activity. This is to ensure that the previously injured area is slowly allowed to recondition to tennis related skills and activities, without overworking them. If return to tennis is too quick then this previously injured area may not be able to tolerate the increased stress, thus lead to re-injury or aggravation. Gradual progressive return to tennis play may involve several factors.

- Upon pain reduction or absence, exercises described in this guide may be safe to attempt. Exercises should be performed with little to no resistance and numbers of repetitions should be reduced to 2 sets of 10 repetitions. If exercises are pain free, repetitions and/or resistance should be safe to increase- GRADUALLY. If exercises are painful, a further reduction in repetitions or resistance, or even cessation of this exercise is required.

- Reducing intensity of tennis play. This may involve reducing the quick movements around the court, simulating strokes without using a ball, hitting against a wall for a more controlled environment, reducing duration of tennis play and reducing force and number of strokes/swings.

- Taking lessons with a tennis professional in order to optimize technique. By using correct techniques it will reduce effort on joints and muscles. This will prevent over stressing and re-aggravation of injury. Poor technique is often the cause of overuse injuries.

- Modifying playing surface. For leg and lower back injuries, playing on clay or grass surfaces will decrease the foot to ground shock, which will further reduce stress to injured areas.

- Modifying equipment. This includes racket, footwear and orthotic devices such as braces, sleeves, and straps. Racket modification may include reducing string tension to lessen vibration and using more a more lightweight racket. Depending on the specific foot problem and unique foot and ankle posture, specific shoes may be required to better position the ankle and foot. Joint or muscle bracing may also be required. Elastic sleeves are generally effective in reducing swelling and providing mild joint support in elbows, knees and ankles. More aggressive bracing is beneficial for more significant joint instability or weakness, such as with ankle and knee sprains. Straps are also helpful in reducing muscle and tendon stress, most commonly with tennis elbow and patellar tendonitis. This equipment may be found at sporting good stores or provided through orthopedic physicians or physical therapists.

- Applying ice for 10 minutes to previously injured body part after tennis or exercise will help to reduce any soreness or potential swelling.

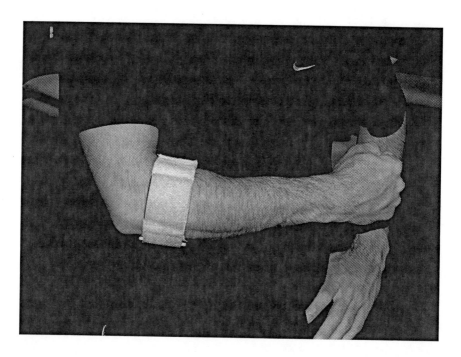

1. Tennis elbow strap: Applies force onto the common extensor tendon of the elbow, which reduces stress along the tendon. This assists with decreasing tendon irritation, thus contributes to improved tissue performance and the healing process.

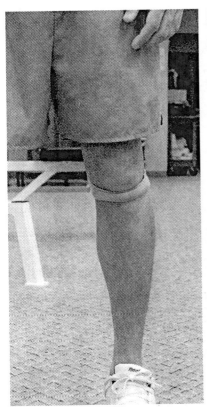 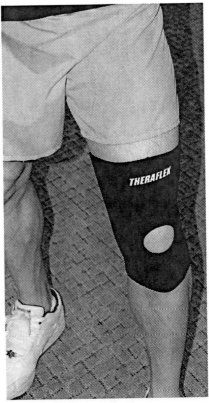

2. Patellar tendon strap: Applies force onto the patellar tendon, which reduces stress onto the tendon. This prevents increased irritation, thus assists with performance and the healing process.

3. Knee sleeve: Provides mild compression to prevent joint swelling, and provides mild support for knee stability.

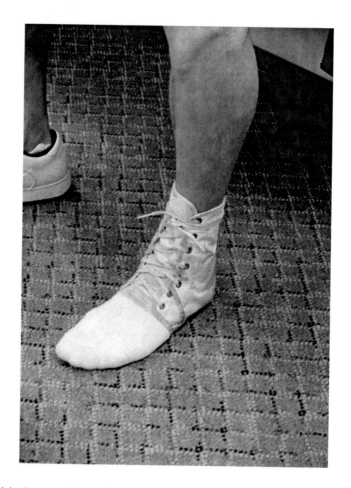

4. Ankle brace: Provides extra side to side stability to the ankle, thus protecting weakened ankle structures.

KEY POINTS TO BETTER TENNIS HEALTH

- Optimize flexibility. This will allow all joints to move through a full necessary motion without restriction.

- Balance strength on all sides of the joint. This will ensure good strength, endurance and stability in joints.

- Perform light warm up and stretching prior to tennis play. This will better prepare muscle and joints for upcoming activity and reduce risk of injury.

- Stretch after tennis play. After tennis, muscles will be warm and more receptive to stretch. Also, it will reduce lactic acid build up and reduce muscle soreness.

- Early injury recognition. Listen to your body. Playing through the pain is not always the right thing to do. Your body is possibly telling you something is wrong.

- Allow for soreness to subside before returning to tennis. This will allow tissues to heal and prevent overstressing.

- Consult a physician when pains persist and do not respond to rest or other simple treatments.

Printed in the United States
132009LV00003B/130/A